WHY TRAIN A DOG ?

A trained dog is a happy dog. Why? Because it brings him into close companionship with his master. The master of a well-trained dog is happy too because he and his dog have found a means of communication. They have reached a basis of mutual respect and understanding.

A dog should be a pleasure, not a problem. One that is spoiled or disobedient can only get himself (and you) into trouble. If he won't sit and stay when you tell him to, or if he won't come instantly when called— well, he may more than likely end up an automobile casualty. A dog that cannot walk on a leash correctly can lead you into trouble on a busy street or in a shop, and the dog who constantly jumps up on people can lose you friends.

Dog training pays dividends in other ways too. For one thing it makes your dog more valuable; more than that, it is the rock bottom on which all dog learning is based. Once the habit of obedience has been ingrained, the number of tricks a dog can be taught is endless.

Your dog's behavior in the house, on the street, in a car; his reactions to strangers; his ability to entertain— all depend on you and the early habits you instill in him.

Training your own dog so that he is a pleasure to live with is the priority of smart owners. Perhaps smarter than his owner is this handsome and happy Border Collie, arguably the most intelligent of all breeds.

It is the purpose of this book to help you do this— to lead you easily step by step through the various training routines, starting with good manners at home, simple obedience training, and a few of the more easily taught tricks, so that you end up with a dog that you will be proud to call your own.

BASIC PRINCIPLES

KNOWING HOW A DOG'S MIND WORKS

The trainer must always keep in mind the limitations of the dog's mind—every dog is an individual. Study your pupil carefully. Adopt methods best suited to his age

Have fun with your dog before and after each session. But when the work begins, be serious. Let him know that you mean business.

Every breed and every dog possesses different mental attributes. Most Huskies are independent, aloof, and of superior intelligence. Trainability varies greatly from dog to dog.

and temperment. A dog does not understand the abstract principles of right or wrong, so reward and punishment are used to teach him what he must or must not do. It is better if one person undertakes the training. During the lessons take the dog away from other pets, children, or activities that might distract him.

TONE OF VOICE

Commands should always be given in a firm voice but there should be no yelling. Your dog will understand the tone of your voice, not the meaning of the word. Your commands should inspire confidence. They should be delivered directly to the dog; not voiced in any haphazard

Unlike children, beginning dogs cannot be taught in classes or groups; however, once the basic principles of training have been ingrained into a dog, group sessions in the hands of a professional trainer are a surmountable challenge.

Affording access to a favorite toy is a viable reward after a training session. This Labrador stops with his favorite Gumabone®.

or hand signals for each exercise so as not to confuse the dog. Repeat the same command over and over until he understands it. At first, hand signals should be exaggerated; as training progresses the exaggeration can be reduced. Use the dog's name when giving commands. Let him master one skill before you try to teach him another. But don't overdo it. Fifteen minutes a day, twice a day, is enough.

REWARD AND PUNISHMENT

When a dog succesfully executes the command, even though his performance has taken more time than desirable, you

In a training class, the instructor can assist or correct the dog's performance. The correct sit position must be straight and balanced.

direction. You can coax a beginner along, but command when you know the dog understands. Demand when you command him to do something and he refuses. The dog must be made to realize that you are boss and that you must and will be obeyed.

CONSTANT REPETITION

Always use the same words and/

should always reward him with at least a pat on the head and warm praise. Dogs are usually anxious to please. They need only to be shown how to do so. When a dog is rewarded for his performance he senses that he has done the right thing and will do it more readily the next time. Reward may take the following forms: kind words, allowing a few minute's romp, patting, allowing the dog to perform his favorite exercise, and treats.

It is not advisable to reward a dog by constantly feeding him tidbits, as he will become accustomed to this form of reward and expect it every time he responds. Every training period must conclude with petting, praise and encouragement to keep up the dog's enthusiasm for his work. If his performance of the particular exercise does not warrant praise, let him perform a short exercise that he has already learned well so that the session can be ended with a legitimate reward.

A correction can be either verbal or physical. Here the trainer is correcting the dog by holding his muzzle.

It is seldom necessary to resort to physical punishment. Withholding praise, using a rebuking tone, or even a reproving "No" are usually punishment enough. But if your dog is callous or insensitive he must be disciplined more severely. Timing is important. The correction, whatever form it takes, must always be administered immediately after the dog misbehaves. His mind cannot connect the punishment with a misdeed committed a few minutes earlier.

Severe punishment should be inflicted only as a last resort, for deliberate disobedience, stubborness, or worst of all, defiance. He must never be punished for clumsiness, slowness in learning, or inability to understand. The word "No" is the indication to the dog that he is doing wrong. "No" is one of the best words to use as a negative command. Speak it in a stern, reproving tone. A handler never slaps a dog with his hand or strikes him with the leash. The hand is used only as an "instrument" of praise and pleasure; the dog must never be allowed to fear it. Strapping a dog with a leash will only make him shy of it and lessen the effectiveness of its legitimate use. Nor is the dog's name ever used when he is being corrected.

If the dog is disciplined when caught in the act of misbehaving, faster results can be expected. Frequently it pays in the long run to withhold disciplinary action until the dog is caught in the act, or to "bait a trap" for him and watch from hiding. By taking advantage of immediate opportunity many a mischievous dog has been cured in one lesson.

PATIENCE

The trainer must never lose patience or become irritated. If he does, the dog will become hard to handle because he will adopt the trainer's attitude. Patience is one of the prime requisites of a good dog trainer, but it must be coupled with firmness. The moment he is sure the dog understands, the handler must insist that the dog obey him. The dog should never be allowed to suspect that there is anything for him to do but obey. He must be made to realize that he will have to do what the trainer commands, that he will eventually have to carry out the command fully, no matter how long it takes. Laxity on the part of the trainer on even one occasion may result in an attitude or mood of disobedience that means difficulty and delay in the continuation of the training program.

A leash correction can be very effective in training an unruly or easily distracted dog.

CHILDREN AND DOGS

A child should have a dog, and it is a good idea to let the child know that the dog is his, and that he is responsible for its care and training. Of course, the parent should supervise, and, if the child is very young, assume those responsibilities which the child can not, however, the child should not realize he is being helped. Let him think he has complete charge.

Many times parents get a dog for their child, turn them loose together without observing them, and let it go at that, saying, "Oh the dog is a natural friend of the child." True, the dog is a natural friend of all humans, big and small, but we must treat him as we would treat a true friend. We do not let our children become unruly in their actions towards their human friends, and we should not let them be anything but considerate to their dog pals.

On the other hand, a puppy, especially if he is of a large breed, needs watching when he first starts playing with a child. Not

Parental supervision of children and dogs, from young puppies to senior dogs, is essential. These two young trainers have been properly instructed to gently handle puppies.

realizing his size and strength, he may jump on a tiny tot and innocently knock him over and rough him up. The child will become frightened after a few bad tumbles and may be wary of dogs for the rest of his life.

Here is where the parent must enter the picture. The dog should be reprimanded and taught the meaning of the word "easy." It is unwise to scold a dog in front of small children. They will try to imitate you. Explain that it is your duty to do the correcting, and that they must not take the task on themselves.

Do not let a child use a dog to pull a wagon, scooter, baby carriage or tricycle unless it is a large breed well over a year old, and a dog harness is used, not a collar. Pulling with a rope attached to a collar puts far too much strain on the animal.

Babies show great interest and fascination in dogs, especially dogs their own size. Always be sure to observe a toddler's interaction with a dog most carefully.

Children should not be allowed to throw a ball into the street or road for the dog to retrieve. This is a dangerous practice. The dog, with his mind on the ball, will dash after it, heedless of oncoming traffic.

A child should not be allowed to throw a stick or ball for a dog to retrieve for any lengthy period of time. The dog can easily become exhausted. This is especially true if the object is thrown into water.

A child's dog should be able to teach him love, kindness, tolerance, consideration, and be a good playmate. In return, the child can teach his pet patience, obedience and loyalty.

If watchfulness and correction are faithfully performed on the part of a parent during the first few months of the child's association with a dog, unlimited harmony will be the result.

ON HIS BEST BEHAVIOR

The training covered in this section is intended to make your dog a good citizen, a member of the family and a friend to all the neighbors. Teaching your puppy the following lessons will also impress on him behavior patterns that will make him more responsive to advanced training.

It is easier to teach a puppy than it is an older dog. Three to four months is the best age to begin. The old saying "You can't teach an old dog new tricks" is only partly true. It should be "An old dog cannot be taught new tricks as quickly as a young dog can."

A puppy has far fewer faults to correct. He has not become set in his ways. He has not been doing the wrong things until they have become established as habits. The older untrained dog has been doing the wrong things all his life, not knowing they were wrong because his faults were never firmly pointed out to him. Making him change his view of life is a more difficult task. It can be done but it requires great patience and persistence.

Food rewards can be introduced to the training sessions right away. Don't overdue it: this is lesson time not lunch time!

Don't overstress a young puppy. While discipline and learning are important, play is as equally necessary, as are rest and affection.

It is extremely important during the first few months of training that you be alert and vigilant to catch the dog the first time he commits an error.

There are those who say "Oh, I want my dog to be natural." This author's reply to that statement is "You can have a natural dog who enjoys all the natural things and still have him obedient." Such habits as chewing on everything in sight, jumping up on furniture, and mussing up visitors may be considered natural by a few but to most of us they represent just plain bad manners.

Never lose your temper or patience when you are teaching your dog. Make him believe by the tone of your voice that you are much more displeased than you really are. Never lose your equanimity; if you do, you will lose control of the situation. A dog soon learns that a master who yells one minute and forgives the next is not to be taken seriously. He knows better than you that you are only letting off steam and do not mean a word you say.

If we are to correct dogs we must prove by our own calm persistence that we are thoroughly qualified to be the boss. Don't let them get away with anything and, to repeat for emphasis, especially not the first or second time. This is particularly true when it comes to disciplining the larger breeds. They must be taught early, while your strength is greater than theirs, that you are in command at all times, and that growling, snapping, or any other kind of resistance, will get them nowhere. Never let your dog dominate you or any member of the family. If you cannot control him, if you cannot make him do what you want him to do, it is better to get rid of him fast!

THOSE FIRST FEW NIGHTS

Not much question about it, the new arrival will be homesick and quite likely to cry. It's probably his first night away from his brothers and sisters, perhaps even his mother. Everything is new and strange. He's lost and trying to let his mother know where he is, not realizing she can't hear him. However, the rapidity with which a pup can be distracted indicates that he's crying not in sorrow but from instinct. So try not to overdo the comforting bit.

When trying to establish a housebreaking routine, the crate is every owner's dream. Dogs naturally take to the crate as their own private place, and instinctively will not soil in their resting place. Be sure the crate is only large enough for the puppy to stand and lay down comfortably.

For the first nights at least, keep his bed within hailing distance so when he cries you can reply with a peremptory "Quiet!" But don't weaken: don't go to him, don't bring him into your room or, even worse, allow him into your bed. Like the camel who begged to stick his nose in the Arab's tent, you may never again be able to keep him out. It is never a good idea to comfort a crying puppy; it gives him the idea that he has only to make noises to gain attention. Better to wait for a period of silence, and then praise him ardently for being a good dog—for being quiet!

There are several time-proven gimmicks you can try. Some owners recommend the use of a wind-up alarm clock. They wrap it in an old towel and put it in the bed, claiming the ticking reminds the pup of his littermates' heartbeats. Another stunt is to wrap a hotwater bottle, two-thirds full of warm water, in a towel, or heat a brick in the oven and put that (well wrapped) in his bed to suggest his mother's warm body. Even a dripping faucet is sometimes effective as a silencer.

Perhaps the best idea is this: just before the pup is put to bed, give him some strenuous exercise to tire him out, and then a dish of warm milk. Natural fatigue will usually take over and he'll fall asleep quickly. Only as a last resort should a sedative or tranquilizer be given, and that should be recommended by a vet. Remember that at its worst night crying never lasts more than a few nights. The puppy stops by himself.

HOUSEBREAKING

Watchfulness is the keynote. Watch your puppy constantly for the first few days after you bring him home. If you live in the country or have a fenced-in yard, let him out the first thing in the morning; for as soon as you begin to show any signs of rising, the puppy will be up and ready for his morning's elimination. Keep your eye on him and as soon as he relieves himself bring him back inside, and praise him. If this is done, he will get the idea that the sooner he performs his duties, the sooner he will get back in the house—and all puppies like to be indoors.

Feed the puppy at scheduled intervals and do not leave dry kibble around during the day. The key to housebreaking a puppy is managing what goes in so as to manage what comes out and when.

In about two hours he will probably want to go again. So try to anticipate his wants. When he starts to sniff around with short, hurried steps, or runs in circles looking for a desirable spot, stop him with a displeased guttural "Ah! Ah!" and put him outside again. Never throw him out or treat him harshly or next time he may sneak around and soil the floor when you are not looking.

If he does elude your watchful eye and commit a nuisance, take him by the loose skin behind the ears and hold him tightly. Hold your temper at the same time. Pull the puppy up to the soiled spot—point to it and say something like "Shame, that isn't nice. Aren't you ashamed!" while you point his nose close to, but not on, the offensive spot. Never rub a dog's nose in his excreta. Let your voice be dramatic with an injured tone in it. Then drag him to the

Training the young puppy to excrete on newspaper is the option of many owners who don't have an easily accessible outdoor area or owners of small toy or terrier dogs.

door by the loose skin, and as you put him out say "Go outdoors when you want to do your business " While it will be too late this time, you are showing him that the proper place is outdoors.

Taking a puppy by the loose skin on the top of his neck does not hurt him physically. It does hurt his feelings, however, and lets him know that you are greatly displeased with his action. The word "Shame!" cannot be interjected too often.

If you are persistent, patient, and watchful, the puppy should be housebroken by the end of a week. Don't forget though that he still has the same number of calls. Let him out as soon as possible in the morning, after each feeding, and just before retiring at night.

Another way to keep a puppy from eliminating indoors, is to put him on a leash and tie him to something rigid—perhaps a screw eye in a baseboard—in an area that he can "call his own." Fold an old blanket and put it there for him to rest on. A puppy will rarely commit a nuisance when tied. You will, of course, continue to release him and take him outside on schedule, remembering always that a puppy has to eliminate on arising, late at night, and ten minutes or so after each feeding.

Still another method of housebreaking is to put the dog in a cage large enough to permit his blanket to be in one end and a spread of newspaper on the other. Four discarded window screens hinged or wired together at the corners make a good temporary cage. The puppy will use the newspaper if necessary, but will

These puppies are certainly too young to housebreak; however, in a few weeks their owner will line half of their bed with newspaper.

soon become disgusted with having his eliminations so close to his bed, and will restrain himself as long as possible until, finally, he will give up using the newspaper altogether. You will, of course, continue to let him out on schedule.

A small breed puppy can be kept in a cage for about six months. You will find it a great convenience. Besides housebreaking him, it will keep him from wandering around the house, getting underfoot, climbing on furniture and chewing on an untold number of household articles. This is not to say that he should be confined constantly. When someone is around to keep an eye on him, he should be allowed play periods in the house and yard—if one is available.

PAPER TRAINING

But alas, there are many of us who have no convenient yard because we live in a city apartment. Here again the cage or "leash to baseboard" method will come in handy. But the dog must also have a definite spot assigned for his eliminations. Spread an area with newspapers. The puppy will gradually show a preference for one spot. Concentrate the papers there. Now follow the same routine as suggested for outdoor training. The spread newspapers take the place of the yard. They should, of course, be removed and destroyed as soon as they are used, but it is a smart idea to leave one soiled sheet behind to remind him of what the paper is for. Housebreaking preparations are available at pet shops to accomplish this same purpose.

When the puppy awakens, and immediately after each feeding, take him to the newspaper and keep him there until he has had his movement; when he has had it, praise him highly. Praise when he does it in the proper place; shame when he does not—these are two more keys to succesful housebreaking.

If you can catch a puppy in the act of misbehaving, so much the better. A scolding then has a longer lasting effect since young dogs do not have good memories. If they are punished some time after a mishap, they do not know what they are being punished for. Always scrub any soiled spots immediately with a strong detergent so that any lingering odor will not attract the dog back to the spot. Ammonia or vinegar are good deodorizers.

STREET TRAINING

When the dog is four months old, street training can formally begin. Some trainers recommend that at this time all newspapers be removed. Others suggest that the newspapers be gradually concentrated in a spot at the outside door, and then under the door, with only one corner of paper showing. When you are walking the puppy on leash, always follow the same route. The dog will soon show a preference for a certain spot. The leash should be long enough to give the dog freedom to sniff about and choose his spot. Smells are important to a dog. Never pull yours away from a good "sniffy" spot unless it is obviously polluted.

Small breeds, particularly toy females, can be trained to use newspapers for life, or a sand- or commercial catlitter box The great danger in this, however, is that being housebound they will not get enough outdoor exercise.

Sometimes a housebroken dog will deliberately show his displeasure when disciplined or left alone by leaving a puddle on your best rug or even on a sofa or bed. The only answer to such an act is extremely firm discipline. A scolding harangue accompanied by a good shaking. Dog authority Blanche Saunders points out that

Pooper scoopers can be purchased from pet shops and pet supply houses. Most cities require owners to clean up after their dogs and only use designated areas.

there are some dogs who when left alone will urinate in the house just for spite, and that on them even the toughest punishment is wasted. They accept their discipline willingly, she believes for the satisfaction of "getting even."

CURBING

When walking a dog your have a civic obligation to your neighbors. He should be taught to use the street, not the sidewalk, nor valuable shrubbery, automobile tires, store fronts, and the like. It is a good idea when walking a dog to keep him in the

Acting courteously at dinnertime is the sign of a well-trained dog. A begging puppy doesn't remain cute for long.

Leaving a dog home with a chew toy can help alleviate destructive behaviors of the bored dog. Rascal spends hours with his favorite Plaque Attacker® bone.

gutter until he has completed his functions, and only then permit him on the sidewalk.

TABLE MANNERS

Some dogs will almost knock their owners down in their haste to get to their food. Such bad manners should be corrected. The "Sit and Stay" commands (discussed later) are useful here. Before the food is placed on the floor the dog should be commanded to sit and stay some distance from the spot. After the food has been put down he should be kept waiting in the "Stay" position with a constant repetition of the command. Only when the handler says "All right" should he be permitted to go to the food.

The best way to avoid the annoyance of a begging dog at the table is to never start passing him bones or table scraps—at least not while you're eating. They should be saved and placed in his regular feeding dish kept in its usual spot. Feed the dog before you eat, or, if his regular feeding time comes later, keep him out of the dining area until the table is cleared. There is nothing more disconcerting to a guest than to watch the family dog eye longingly every mouthful he puts into his mouth.

CHEWING

A puppy from three to six months old is anxious to test his on a big bone than your upholstered sofa. So giving him his own chewable toys to play with will lessen the chances of his going to work on your household treasures.

It is wrong to encourage a mischievous puppy by condoning his misbehavior regardless of how cute he looks. This sometimes happens when he chews on something of no value: he looks appealing

Dogs naturally need to chew. Provide safe chew toys such as Nylabones® or Gumabones® or hard, delectable treats such as Chooz®. This German Shepherd is contentedly supping on his chicken and cheese flavored Chooz®.

teeth and exercise his jaws on just about everything he sees. Sometimes, too, excessive chewing is the result of a vitamin deficiency, and a vitamin-mineral formula added to to puppy's daily diet will be the only remedy needed.

Contrary to what you may think, the pup would rather chew chewing on that old shoe that you were going to throw out anyway. Laugh now and you will be shouting "bad dog" later on when he ruins a brand new pair of shoes. This can lead only to a confused, undisciplined puppy.

Approval or disapproval of whatever he is chewing on can be shown in your voice. When he chews on his things, give him a rewarding "Good boy" but when he chews on yours, an emphatic "No, leave it alone!" accompanied by a loud noise, such as clapping your hands, shaking a tin can filled with stones or coins, or banging two pots together, will stop him in mid-action. A banishment to isolation for a short time may follow.

Make sure that everyone in the family does this consistently. Training is wasted if one member of the family is permissive while the others are not.

If the damage has already been done when you discover it, show him the chewed object and scold him, letting him see the destruction, and how much his destructiveness has grieved you. Make him feel contrite, and then banish him. Later, test him. Leave the article within his reach but stand by, concealed. If and when he starts for it, startle him with a loud noise and a sharp "Leave it alone!" from your place of concealment. Frequently such warnings coming from an unseen source cause the dog to believe that he is constantly being watched.

As in the case of old shoes, it is unwise to give a puppy any discarded household article or piece of clothing for a plaything. Obviously puppies cannot distinguish new from old. This is particularly true of objects made of leather. If the dog does grab onto something and won't loosen his grip, snap your fingers against his nostrils and command "Drop it!"

If chewing persists try sprinkling the articles he particularly favors with a strong solution of bitter aloes, or a sprinkling of red hot pepper (not Paprika or Tabasco sauce). Repellant sprays, specially made for this purpose, are available in petshops.

Large beef bones make excellent toys and teethers; however, natural bones are very abrasive and should be used sparingly. On the market there are many kinds of synthetic chewable bones and toys made from such things as annnealed nylon and polyurethane. There are a great variety of Nylabone® products available that veterinarians recommend as safe and healthy for your dog or puppy to chew on. All in all, balls probably make the best playthings. Their rolling and bouncing seem to give them a life of their own, of which a puppy never appears to tire.

Nylabone®products come in many shapes and sizes, from bones to balls. The Gumaball® will be any puppy's favorite toy to chase.

Adult dogs never outgrow of their love for Nylabone® products. This handsome Irish Setter poses with his Plaque Attacker® bone. Nylabones® are recommended by trainers and veterinarians alike as dental devices to keep teeth clean and as stress releasers to keep dogs healthy in mind and spirit.

FURNITURE-BREAKING

Housebreaking is, of course, your pup's first lesson and by now you should be well on your way with that. Furniture-breaking can go along with it; that is, if you want to keep your pup off beds, chairs and sofas. Some people don't care, that is, they don't care until it's too late to break the grown dog of this bad habit.

Naturally, your pup loves the easy life. He thinks that comfortable chair or sofa is meant Or, if a newspaper isn't at hand at the critical moment, toss an old book or magazine at his side. Don't hit him—startle him! Balancing a metal tray of empty cans on the arm of a chair or sofa sometimes works. When he jumps the tray falls on the floor with a noisy clatter.

He'll catch on quickly if you and every member of the family keep at it. But that's the trick—keeping at it. Being permissive one time and forbidding the next will get you nowhere. Dog repellant

The house rules must be established during puppyhood. It is nearly impossible to teach the adult dog not to do something he's enjoyed throughout his puppyhood.

for him too, when he sees how much you enjoy it. He's intrigued too by that interesting scent you leave behind. It's up to you to teach him his proper place. First of all, if he has a comfortable spot of his own, he'll less likely to want yours. A stern "No!" emphasized with the crack of a rolled-up newspaper will point out his error. sprays are useful for this too. They smell bad to him, but not to you and are harmless when directions are followed.

NEEDLESS BARKING

If your pup barks when he is left alone, your neighbors will let you know about it in no uncertain terms. Their complaints are usually justified so break your little darling of this bad habit before the law steps in and says "keep him quiet or give him up!"

You cannot begin training a puppy to remain alone too early. This is why crating him, or at least shutting him up in a small room during the formative months, has been recommended. Even if someone is home all day, there should be lengthy periods when the puppy is made to stay alone while his whines or barks are either, if possible, completely ignored, or silenced with an occasional shouted "Quiet!" Strict discipline in the early months will pay off in big dividends later. When your neighbors inform you that your dog barks constantly in your absence you will have to

Some dogs are relentlessly barky. Be stern from puppyhood and don't tolerate needless barking. Of course, if your dog is trying to warn you of danger by barking, reward him for being a good watchdog.

Outdoor dogs can be a nuisance to neighbors if unnecessarily barking. It's best to handle this situation before it becomes a severe problem.

embark on a strict program of disciplinary training. Dress yourself as if you were going to be away for some time. Let the dog hear your receding footsteps. If you usually drive away in a car you will have to get in the car, drive a short distance, and return quietly on foot, making sure that the dog cannot hear you, always remembering that his hearing is far keener than yours. Chances are he'll start to bark as soon as he thinks you are gone. The moment he starts, bellow out a sharp "No !" or "Quiet !" and rush back inside, scolding fiercely and making a great display of bad temper. Some trainers recommend splashing a cup of water in the dog's face, or using a water pistol or spray bottle.

A few lessons like this, before the habit becomes deeply ingrained, should teach any puppy that his howling will only result in an angry master.

However, some older larger breeds of dogs with confirmed habits may require more strenuous action. When you rush back inside, grab his collar and strap his haunches, scolding all the time. (Never punish a dog by striking out at him or chasing him around the house with a stick). Hold him and shake him, while you scold him.

It is wise, of course, when leaving a puppy alone, to confine him to a crate or bathroom. You should make sure that he is comfortable, has plenty of fresh, clean drinking water and some of his toys to play with, and that he will not miss a feeding time. A mature dog, once trained, can be given the run of the house to act as watchdog.

The methods of stopping a dog from barking vary greatly. Most trainers advocate "anything that works." Be imaginative, surprise your misbehaving howler with a trick of your own.

A dog fenced in a yard who barks at everything and everybody can usually (in warm weather only) be disciplined by a pail of water tossed over him every time he barks. You must, of course, be waiting out of sight until the barking begins, and then rush out shouting "No . . . Quiet !" and dash the water over him. Fill the bucket and return to your watchful waiting. Repeat until no longer necessary . . . perhaps as many as 30 times. The essential thing is to make the penalty outweigh the pleasure.

QUIET!

You will not, of course, condemn a dog for barking at strangers. It is in his nature to warn off intruders. He should be taught, however, to cease barking at your command. Call "Quiet!" then hold his mouth closed. At first he will not understand and as soon as you let go will resume barking. Don't be discouraged.

Hold his mouth closed and repeat the command over and over until he begins to catch on.

Many dogs develop strong prejudices against milkmen, mailmen, and delivery men. It is to your advantage to introduce your dog to these routine callers, talking to them pleasantly in the muzzle. Shut the dog in a small room. When he begins bark go into the room and put his muzzle on him. Leave, shutting the door behind you, and let hem remain alone for from 30 minutes to an hour. Return, remove the muzzle, and hang it on the door at a spot where the dog can see, but not

One of the oldest tricks in the book: the water bucket is a surprise your noisy pooch won't forget. Remember to use COLD water.

dog's presence, so that he will come to regard them as friends.

A dog who barks a warning is a valuable companion but a yapper who barks at everything is a nuisance unless he is taught to stop on command.

Inside the house, a constant yapper can be disciplined by severe scolding and expulsion into another room—alone. If, when let out, he resumes his barking, a quick re-internment is called for.

Another training device is the reach it. Go away and wait for the dog to start barking again. Return, take the muzzle down, and put it back on the dog. Repeat until the dog realizes that he will be muzzled if he doesn't remain quiet when left alone.

If he has a habit of barking needlessly at night, feed him his big meal as late as possible because a stuffed belly often has a quieting effect.

Obedience training becomes invaluable in controlling the barking dog. It can help a lot because it makes the dog understand that he must obey on command. When he is well trained in obedience he will stop barking when ordered to, no matter what the occasion, be it barking when the doorbell rings, when a visitor approaches, or when about to be left behind.

JUMPING ON PEOPLE

Start early correcting your dog of the bad habit of jumping on people in boisterous greeting. There is no excuse for putting up with this annoyance. It is particularly unfair to guests.

His first jumping will, of course, be directed toward you and members of the family. There are several things you can do. When he jumps, grab hold of his front paws and fling him away; at the same time call a firm "Down!" Or

With a dog as large as an Akita, jumping up can be a serious problem. Try lightly bumping your knee at the dog's chest to discourage this behavior.

try raising your foot as he rears up so that he bumps against it.

With big dogs it is a good idea to raise your knee sharply, timing your action so that he bumps your knee as he leaps upon you. Give a gentle thrust so that he falls backward. Do this every time he jumps and make sure that every member of your family does it too. Instruct your close friends that when they call they are to do the same.

Be consistent. Never let a dog jump up when you are wearing old clothes, and then expect him not to when you arrive home wearing your Sunday best.

It is, of course, not possible to correct a dog every time he jumps, but the more frequently you can correct it the better.

MAKE OBEDIENCE A HABIT

Public acceptance of the dictum that "an obedient dog is a joy forever" is undoubtedly the reason why Obedience Trials have now become the most popular branch of competitive dog sports. It is somewhat surprising, however, to learn that formal obedience training for dogs, and competitive trials, did not begin in this country until 1934 with a single class of eight dogs in Bedford Village, New York. It was started by Mrs. Whitehouse Walker of Mt. Kisco, New York, who brought back the idea from England.

The principal value of obedience training, however, is not that it promotes the Obedience Trial as a sport but that it brings home to all of us the fact that it is a simple and easy matter to teach dogs of all breeds, mongrels included, to obey commands readily and willingly. Anyone who wants to teach his pet the simple niceties of behavior in order to make him a more pleasant

In training classes, the instructor can demonstrate proper and effective ways to correct the dog's bad habits.

companion and a more valuable animal, need only visit an obedience training class. After watching for a session or two he will be convinced that anyone of even temper and reasonable patience can teach his own dog these commands.

The basic need of the average owner, especially in the cities, is to train his dog to come when called, to cease tugging at the end of the leash when out for a walk, to stop unnecessary barking, to refrain from jumping up on visitors, and to sit and stay when told.

Most owners who enter their dogs in training classes enter primarily to seek help on these points. But they then continue on to learn all of the Companion Dog routines (the Novice course), and a good percentage of them go even further to see how well their dogs do in competitions where relatives and friends can watch them perform.

While there are five classes in the organized Obedience Trials, there are only three divisions of schooling: The Novice Class, which leads to the Companion Dog degree (CD); the Open Class, which brings the Companion Dog Excellent honor (CDX.); the Utility Class, which wins the Utility Dog title (UD), and the Utility Dog Excellent title (UDX).

Within the limitations of this book only those exercises taught in the beginning, or Novice Class, can be discussed. Those owners who wish to continue on to more advanced training are advised to consult other books on the subject.

There are six exercises in the Novice Class. They are Heel on Leash, Stand for Examination, Heel Free (Off Leash), Recall (Come When Called), the Long Sit (lasting one minute) and the Long Down (three minutes). These last two exercises must be done with all the dogs in the ring together, but with their handlers at the opposite side.

Placing the leash on the puppy will tell him that he's going to receive attention, whether in the form of a walk or a training session.

Although most trainers believe that dogs should be nine months to a year old before enrolling in class, it is generally acknowledged that the most important factor is how the temperament of the individual dog is suited to the work.

In the pages that follow you will be taught a few early puppy commands as well as the elementary exercises which your dog must know to win the degree of Companion Dog in a formal obedience training class. But even if you never intend to go in for more formal training, you will find these lessons invaluable in controlling your dog at all times—at home and in public—and increase your pleasure in being with your canine companion.

PUPPY WALKING

Teaching a puppy to walk on a leash is not difficult. First get him used to his new collar by letting him wear it around the house for a little while each day, gradually lengthening the periods until he forgets that it's there. Then tie a short streamer of rag to it—an old necktie will do—and let him drag it around the house. At first he will tug at it but before long he'll get used to the idea of something dangling from his neck.

Next substitute a short leash for the rag. Let him drag this around the house (and yard, if you have one) on leash, but *letting him lead you,* and coaxing him along. When he is used to this, take him on the sidewalk for his first venture.

Double check his collar before you take him out. If it's on too tight it will choke him; if it's too loose it

The proper way to place a choke collar around a dog's neck. Be sure to align the loops up correctly or else the collar cannot perform its function.

the house; under supervision, of course, because he is likely to chew the leather or catch the handle on some protruding object that could choke him. The next step is to parade him around the will slip over his head and, in panic, he may run away.

Your pup should walk on your left side; hold the leash in your right hand, but control it with your left.

Professional trainer demonstrating the hand signal for stay. The dog is working on lead and the trainer is not using voice commands with the hand signal. This is an intermediate level of training.

Call your puppy's name and start walking He will quickly discover that it is useless to struggle and more comfortable to stay close enough to keep the leash slack. When he does walk quietly at your side praise him extravagantly and stroke his muzzle.

HAND SIGNALS

It is wise to use hand signals along with voice signals from the very beginning. It will not be long before the dog learns to respond to the gesture alone, and the vocal command can be dispensed with. This is quite impressive when displaying your dog's achievements to friends and neighbors but, in addition, it has a more practical use. Hand signals are used in formal Obedience Trials.

TO COME WHEN CALLED (RECALL)

Fasten a collar with a 20-foot leash attached to it around the puppy's neck. A length of light clothesline or venetian blind cord can be substituted if a long leash is not available. Have reward tidbits (yummies or small slices of cooked frankfurter are good for this) in your pocket. Shorten the leash by coiling it in your hand. Walk away from the puppy and call his name. Speak the command in a calm, decisive tone. Say "Rover, come here!" as you jerk lightly on the leash. If he does not come repeat the command and jerk easily but persistently on the leash as you coil up the slack and pull the puppy to your feet. Say "Good dog" in a pleased tone, give him a bite to eat, and pet him.

Now go the full length of the leash away and repeat. Do this eight or ten times. Repeat the lesson three times a day if possible. After two or three days of this, the puppy will more than likely come the instant you call. Never jerk unnecessarily hard on the leash when taking in the slack—just enough to be effective. Your object is to teach him his name and the meaning of "Come here!" In formal obedience training this exercise is known as the Recall, and this hand signal is generally used: Let the right hand hang loosely, palm-out, at your side. Bring it up in a wide sweeping gesture diagonally across your body to end palm-up at your left shoulder.

SIT AND STAY

Put the training leash and collar on the puppy, and reward tidbits in your pocket. Hold him on

The trainer is using the hand signal for come (also called recall). This Samoyed is working off lead but the trainer is still using voice commands in conjunction with the hand signals.

a short length of leash, the rest of it coiled in your hand. Say "Sit" and press lightly with your hand on his hindquarters until you have him in the correct position. Repeat "Sit" all the time you are seating him. After you have him seated, remove your hands from his body, and say repeatedly "Stay." Let your "Stay" be spoken in a tone intended to steady him. If he should start to get up, press him back into the sitting position, repeating "Sit" until he is seated once more. Repeat "Stay" as you slowly remove your hands.

When he has held the position for a few seconds without the pressure of your hand, say "All right!" in a pleased tone. Pull him close to your feet, give him his reward and a pat of approval. Repeat the process for the usual ten minutes of lesson time, and give the lesson several times a day. Each day get farther away from the puppy while you continue to keep him sitting by your "Stay."

Always pull him to you for his reward after you give the "All right" as a sign that you are pleased. Soon the puppy will come for his reward without the pull, but make him wait for your "All right."

Now as a final step, lay the leash

Demonstrating the down/stay with a well-trained Akita, this trainer is using only hand signals to communicate with the dog. Akitas are among the most difficult of all breeds to train because they are very headstrong and independent by nature.

on the ground as you back away from the dog, and when you reach the end lay it on the ground and back off as far as possible, repeating the admonition "Stay" every time he appears about to break.

The hand signal for "Sit" is to hold the hand straight down in front of you, slightly extended with the elbow rigid. The signal is given with fingers and wrist. The fingers are flicked downward without closing the hand.

The signal for "Stay" is as follows: Extend your slightly cupped hand towards the dog's muzzle as if you were going to squeeze his nose. Stop just short of touching him and hold the hand there for a moment.

DOWN AND STAY

Make the puppy sit and stay. Gently pull his front feet out from under him and press on his shoulder as you say "Lie down!" See that he strikes a natural, comfortable position. To lie down naturally, most dogs lie on one side of their hindquarters, with the body slightly curved towards the front feet, which are straight out.

Golden Retriever perfectly illustrates the sit/stay for his trainer. Although Golden Retrievers have a reputation for being less than bright, they consistently prove the most trainable and obedient of all dogs.

Above: Professional trainer demonstrating the stay hand signal while dog is in the down position.
Below: Bulldog in the sit position. The dog should be sitting directly in front of the handler in the correct position.

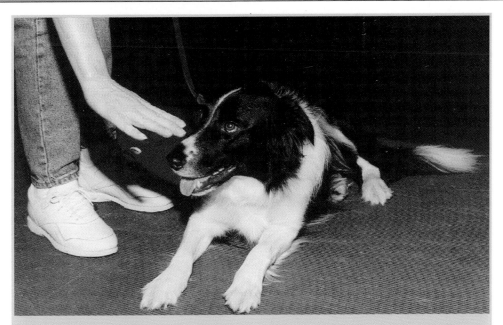

Above: Border Collie in the down/stay position. The hand signal for this position is to raise the arm to shoulder height and bring it down in a fast striking motion, hand spread as if you were to push the dog down.
Below: German Wirehaired Pointer performing the recall exercise in obedience class. This hand signal is to let your right hand hang loosely at your side, palm-out. Bring it up in a wide sweeping gesture diagonally across your body to end palm-up at your left shoulder.

Continue to say "Down" while placing him. When he is placed properly say "Stay" while you stand up. If he starts to act up, anticipate his actions, and say sharply "Down! Down!" When he has held his position for several seconds, give him the now familiar "All right" in a light, pleased tone, and reward him.

After he has held his position several times, give him "Down" without aiding him. If he does not respond, pretend that you are going to pull his front feet out while you repeat "Down," but do not help him unless absolutely necessary.

When he lies down by himself, back away to the end of the leash as you continue to say "Stay!"

The hand signal for "Down" is to raise the arm to shoulder height and bring it down in a fast striking motion, hand spread as if you were to push the dog down. "Stay": the same signal used for "Sit" and "Stay."

HEELING

There is a lot of difference between correct leash walking—heeling as it is called in the dog world—and just "walking the dog." Heeling means graceful progress with the dog walking close to your left heel with his nose on a line with your knee, his head erect, his manner eager. He should pull neither right nor left, neither back nor forth, always adapting his pace to yours.

When heeling, the handle and excess slack of the leash are held in your right hand. The thong should pass across your body to the dog who should be on your left. You control the leash with your left hand, shortening or lengthening it as necessary.

Say cheerfully and clearly "Rover, heel" and step out with your left foot. Don't look at the dog. Appear to take it for granted that he will trot beside you.

Soft Coated Wheaten Terrier in the down position. The dog should be in a natural, comfortable position, with the feet straight out in front.

When he doesn't, when he strains ahead, jerk back sharply with your left hand, but let the leash slacken instantly. Each time repeat the command "Heel." Never pull the dog back into position and never drag him; it accomplishes nothing. The quick jerk is what does it. It makes the dog momentarily uncomfortable and he quickly learns that if he walks

German Wirehaired Pointer heeling on a lead. The dog should be walking close to your left heel with his nose on a line with your knee, his head erect, and his manner eager.

correctly there will be no jerk. Always jerk the lead in the opposite direction than the dog is moving, never straight up. If the dog barges ahead, jerk backwards; if he lags, jerk forward. When you snap the lead the correct way, you will hear the collar click.

Keep walking, keep jerking when necessary, and keep repeating "Heel!" Patting your left leg every so often sometimes helps. Remember to praise him after each return to position. A good way if he is not too small, is to gently touch his nose with your left palm and tickle him under the chin.

Another method is to practice this exercise alongside a straight wall. Each time that the dog tries to pass, crowd him against the wall to stop him.

Whenever you come to a halt, order the dog to "Sit" at your left heel. Before long he will do this voluntarily, and no command will be needed.

TURNS

At first, turning will present a problem: you will both have to remember something for this. Just before you make a left turn, get the dog's attention with a "Heel!" and at the same time tighten up on the leash with your left hand and hold it away from your body to keep him from bumping into you. Turn on your left foot, bring the right foot around in the new direction. If he tangles into you, say "Heel" sharply, bump him with your knee and this, with the jerk, should remind him what to do. A turn to the right is much the same, only this time the dog has farther to travel. Turn on your

right foot, swing your left and, saying "Heel," circle the dog around on a taut leash.

When he has mastered simple heeling, vary the pace. Walk fast and slowly, change frequently, and always make him maintain the proper position. Using two friends as posts, or even two chairs set eight to ten feet apart, start from midway between them and walk around one, cross back and walk around the other to return to the starting point following a figure-eight path.

You will know your dog has learned to heel properly when you can walk in different places with the end of the leash slung loosely over your shoulder. If he makes a dash, step on the leash to bring him up short. When he will heel like this, teach him to heel when off the leash completely. Then, wherever you go, he'll always be trotting at your left side.

OFF THE LEAD (HEEL FREE)

Once your dog is first allowed off the leash, something is sure to attract his attention and he'll dash off. If he's learned to come when called, your job is much easier. Otherwise retrieve him in any way you can. It's usually better to wait for the dog to return either from choice or enticement than to chase him. If you run after him, he'll think it's a game and run away. However, if you casually walk away chances are he'll follow. Put the leash back on and continue with an "on leash" lesson, praising him when he's done well, scolding him when his attention wanders. Remember

Australian Shepherd heeling. Once your dog has mastered simple heeling, vary the pace. Walk fast and slowly, change frequently and always make him maintain the proper position.

German Shepherds stand for examination. This position is also called stacking and dogs must remain in this stance for long periods of time when they are in the show ring.

that it's easier to train a dog to walk off leash if he's already mastered the command "Come!" But many people have trained their dogs to heel so well that they never have to use any comands.

Hand signal: Use a forward motion of the left hand parallel to the ground.

STAND FOR EXAMINATION

If your dog has learned his "Sit" lesson well, he will start to sit as soon as you stop heeling him. Put your arms around him, command "Stand!" and bring him to his feet. It may be necessary to actually pose him by lifting him a little off his feet and then setting him squarely down on them. Keep repeating the command "Stand!" Finally, when he holds the pose, walk around in front of him and remain there for a few seconds. Do not let him relax into the "Sit" position. Continue hoisting him to his feet and commanding "Stand!" until he assumes a statuesque pose every time you tell him to. Even if you never show your dog to a judge in competition, the poise and sureness he will gain from this exercise make it well worth teaching him.

Sit is the most comfortable position for a dog to be in when shaking hands. Remember to always praise and reward your dog for a job well done.

YOUNG DOGS—OLD TRICKS

In this section we cover those tricks that, while not always useful in themselves are highly entertaining. If his earlier training has been given correctly your dog will by now enjoy learning new things and look forward to his lessons. It's fun to put a dog through his tricks before an audience and both you and, believe it or not, he will welcome the applause.

By putting something sweet on your cheek, such as syrup or jelly, you can easily teach your dog to kiss on command. Adults should always supervise children and dogs, especially when teaching this trick.

Remember that it may be an old trick to you, but to your puppy it's new so start with the easy ones first—those that do not put too much of a strain on his still-strengthening muscles.

SHAKE HANDS

Puppies instinctively paw at each other in play. Your pup will paw at you. Fine. Grab the paw and say "Shake!" Wrong paw? Most probably, since puppies usually extend the paw nearest to the hand you're using. With the dog in the "Sit" position, push against his right shoulder with your left hand. As his right foot comes up, take it in your right hand, shake, then praise and reward. Keep repeating the command "Shake hands" until he responds every time. After he has learned to shake "right-handed," teach him to shake with the left paw on a slightly different command: "Other hand" for instance.

KISS ME

Hold the dog close to your cheek and say "Give me a kiss!" He may have been eager to kiss you without the command, but this cue identifies the word "kiss" with the action. If he becomes too affectionate, restrain him with "That's enough!" but do not let him think that all kissing is taboo.

If your pet is shy about kissing

A popular trick is to teach your dog to roll over from one side to the other in a 180-degree arc on command, as gracefully portrayed by this Standard Poodle.

each time and wait for him to bark. Return at once, say "Speak," and reward him. Do not reward him if he merely yelps or whines.

An excitable dog can usually be induced to bark by playing with him, speaking excitedly in a high pitched voice or showing him a tidbit, allowing him to smell it and then holding it beyond his reach.

Once he has learned to identify the word "Speak" with barking, he will respond to your command by barking. The last step is to put him on leash to keep him in a sitting position when he "speaks." If you do not insist on making him sit, he will acquire the habit of jumping around while working up a bark.

(this is rare) put a dab of syrup or jelly on your cheek. After a few rehearsals he'll kiss without this added attraction. "Kiss my hand" can be taught in the same way.

If there is another member of the family who has no objection to being kissed, put the dog on a short leash and say "Go to her . . .him" . . .or use the person's name: "Go to Ann!" and as Ann bids him welcome with a beckoning "Come" lead the dog to her and say "Put your feet up" and, that done, add "Give Ann a kiss" as she lowers her cheek.

SPEAK

Teaching a dog to speak on command is not difficult. Simply get him to associate the word "Speak" with the act of barking. Every time he barks naturally, encourage it, and, repeat "Speak! Speak!" For more formal training confine him to a spot he does not like. Have some treats handy. Every time he barks, say "That's it, speak" and give him a treat and encouraging praise.

If he barks only when you are out of sight, absence yourself

ROLL OVER

Rolling over on command will come easy if your dog has already learned "Down" and "Stay." Get him in the down position, hold him there for a moment or two and then say "Roll over!" Illustrate your meaning by taking hold of his front feet and rolling him from

Although your dog should be in the down position when teaching him to roll over, this acrobatic Bull Terrier starts his roll from a standing position.

one side to the other as you repeat the command. Do this a few times as a preliminary exercise. Rolling him by hand can soon be eliminated.

Just as a dog will watch your finger when you're teaching him to beg, his eyes will follow a treat half-hidden in your hand. Hold it beyond his nose and arch your hand from extreme left over his body to the floor on his extreme right. As his neck is not double jointed, to follow the treat in your one hand he will have to roll over in a 180-degree arc Keep one hand on his body to prevent his jumping up. Praise and reward.

If he insists on getting up to get the treat, lay him on his back and grip a leg in each hand. Roll him over from one side to the other, repeating the command.

Use whatever method that works best for you and your dog when teaching tricks. This handler has developed her own special hand signal for teaching her Bichon Frise to play dead.

When he finally does roll on command, even half correctly, give him the treat. But if he rolls over of his own accord before you tell him to, do not reward him since we want to associate the treat with the verbal command. Show your annoyance by a stern "No . . . No." Put him in the "Down-Stay" position and start over. Never keep him at it for more than 15 minutes at a time, and never end the lesson without a reward.

PLAYING DEAD

Playing dead, playing possum, or "Go to sleep" are different names for the same pointless but harmless trick that dogs seem to enjoy. Any dog who has learned "Down" can be taught to "Play Dead" quickly. Give the command "Down" and then say sadly "Dead dog" or "Play Possum" or "Go to sleep" —whichever you prefer, but choose one and stick to it—and at the same time roll the dog over on his side with his head flat down. Keep him that way for a moment, soothing him by stroking him gently. Keep repeating the command. When he relaxes, take your hands away but keep on repeating. Release him with an "All right" or "Okay."

If he has not yet learned "Down" make your dog lie on his side and soothe him by stroking him gently before repeating the chosen command.

His natural tendancy will be to

raise his head and look around. But hold him in the correct position as you repeat. Gradually the length of time can be extended. Be generous with your praise when he performs well.

PUT YOUR FEET UP

Keep the dog on a short leash when you begin teaching this lesson. Use a box, chair, or low table. Say "Put your feet up" and point to the box. He may try to jump up on it but if he does, restrain him with the leash. Show him what you mean by placing his front feet on the box. Tell him to "Stay!" If he tries to sit down while holding his front feet on

A wooden dumbbell, like the one this Beagle has retrieved, is a popular training device in obedience training. The size and weight of the dumbbell you use should vary with the size of the dog.

the box, raise him to the proper position. When he holds it, give him your cheery "All right" and a small treat as a reward. When he starts getting used to the idea, back farther and farther away, repeating "Stay." After a few moments release him with an "All right" and make him come to you for his reward.

Now add the word "box" to the command: "Put your feet up on the box." Later on you can gradually add other objects to his repertoire: "Put your feet up on the bed... the chair... the stool... the table, etc." and before long he will be able to distinguish among them.

FETCH AND CARRY

Here's a way to exercise your dog but still take it easy yourself. Throw a ball and have him bring it back to you—and throw it again, and again. Any dog worth his salt will go after a ball (or any other object) when you throw it, but he will not necessarily, unless trained, bring it back to you. As you throw the ball, say "Fetch ball!" When he has it in his mouth say "Fetch." Have some treats in your pocket. As he gets near you, drop a treat on the ground at your feet. Say "Drop it." When he sees the reward he'll head for it, dropping the ball, in order to eat the treat. Let him enjoy it, and then throw the ball again.

Teaching your dog to catch a Frisbee®* is great exercise.
*The trademark Frisbee is used under license from Mattel, Inc., California, USA.

By substituting other objects for the ball and calling "Fetch stick! . . . Fetch newspaper! . . . Fetch basket! . . . Fetch bag!" etc., he will quickly learn to differentiate among them, and at the same time begin to learn the associate command "Carry" when the dog is to carry the object as he walks beside you.

To accomplish "Carry," when he retrieves the object and brings it to you, say "Carry" and back away a little. He will follow. After a few

PICK IT UP AND HANG ON TO IT

Lay a stick or wooden dumbbell on the ground or floor in front of the dog, and say "Pick it up!" Insist upon obedience. If he does not pick it up, press his head towards the object, then open his mouth and place it across his jaws. Close his mouth and repeat "Hang on to it!" with your hand under his chin to make sure that he does. After he has held it for a few moments, either with or without your help,

This Border Collie is returning a Gumadisc® to his handler. This polyurethane disc is soft and floppy, and pet shops guarantee that it will last ten times longer than cheap plastic discs.

steps take the object, and give him a reward. Each time you move away, make the distance longer, turning finally so that the dog is walking normally at your side before you relieve him of the object by saying "Drop it !" After a few lessons, instead of throwing the object, just point to it and say "Pick up the ball... bag... basket..." or whatever, and when he has done so, add "Carry" and start walking.

say "Drop it!" Repeat until he will pick up the object without having it forced into his mouth.

The entire routine of "Pick it up," "Hang on to it," "Carry," and "Drop it" will probably take several weeks to perfect.

TAKE IT TO HIM

Have your dog on a leash, and a willing assistant sitting down. Tell the dog to pick up one of his

The Gumabone® Frisbee®* has the advantage of a dog bone molded on the top, making it easier for the dog to pick up.
*The trademark Frisbee is used under license from Mattel, Inc., California, USA.

favorite playthings. Lead him to the person you want to accept it. When the dog gets here say "Put your feet up" indicating the person's lap. When he puts his feet up, say "Drop it!" Reward, and repeat the action.

Later, go a few feet away from the person and send the dog on the same mission. Say "Take it to him !" Add "Put your feet up ... Drop it!" Never let him drop the object until he is told to.

Later you can give him other objects to carry and send him to different people.

CATCH IT

Use a soft ball of catchable size. Command your dog to sit and stay. Work close to him. Tell him to "Catch it" as you toss the ball from a few inches in front of his nose. Chances are he'll miss or make no attempt to catch it the first few times. He may run to it after it falls on the ground. This is what you want to prevent. Stop with a "No No! Stay!" and make him stay in position while you retrieve the ball.

Try again and always pretend to be highly annoyed if he misses. When he finally starts catching the easy tosses, gradually work farther away until the time comes that he catches them all. Then start varying the objects you throw—a knotted rag, a round of wood, or a string-tied wad of newspaper are good substitutes.

If he shows reluctance, toss him small treats until he gets your meaning, but never let him eat a tidbit unless he catches it. If he shows no interest at all in catching, try this: Fasten a favorite treat on a string. Dangle this "bait" over his head and say "Catch it." If he doesn't snatch at it, swing it away and repeat. If he does catch it, let him eat the treat. Gradually swing the bait higher over his head so he'll have to jump for it. Every time repeat "Catch it." When he never misses, discard the string and start tossing the treat from a distance. When he's sure-fire, substitute the ball.

BACK UP

Bring the dog up short on a leash with the rest of it coiled in your hand so that it will pay out easily. Motion with your free hand, palm-out, in a gesture that naturally implies

An Australian Cattle Dog successfully catches a ball. Make sure the ball that you use is soft and of catchable size, not too big and definitely not too small.

With a lot of patience and practice your dog can be good enough to enter organized competitions. Border Collie catching a Frisbee®*.
*The trademark Frisbee is used under license from Mattel, Inc., California, USA.

"Back up!" Repeat the words "Back up!" with each hand motion.

Shuffle your feet up until they touch the dog's front paws. It will sometimes be necessary to step lightly on his toes. By shuffling along and touching the dog's toes, he will back away from the contact of your feet. As soon as he takes a backward step or two, encourage him with "Good boy" and reward him.

After a little repetition of your foot action, it will be unnecessary to use it further. The dog will understand what "Back up" means from your words and motions.

It is a good idea to alternate spoken words with hand action, so that the pup will react to either. Later he will then "Back up" with just the gesture.

CRAWL

With the dog on a long leash, give him his cue, "Down!" Now say in a calm tone "Come on... Crawl!" and pull gently on the leash. If he starts to rise to his feet, say quickly "No! No! Down! Crawl!" You may have to press him down if he tries to get up. "Come!" or "Come here!" may have to be replaced with "Crawl" to get him to creep towards you, but use the word "Crawl" as often as possible.

Work close to your dog. Keep backing away from him until he learns the meaning of "Crawl."

After that you can send him to a given spot and let him crawl to you while you stand still. Assign the dog his starting place. Show it to him the first few times you give this part of the lesson. Then say "Go back there !" after he has crept to your feet. You can encourage him to go to his starting place with these words, "Go on! . . . Keep going! . . . Over there! . . . No! No !" until he reaches the right spot. When he gets there say "That's it . . . Stay!" and then repeat the lesson.

Later, you can teach him to crawl through improvised tunnels and around various obstacles.

The Gumabone® Tug Toy allows a dog and his owner to have a game of tug-of-war. The owner grips one end while the dog grips the other—then they pull. The polyurethane flexible tug toy is the best on the market; they are clear in color and stay soft forever.

TUG-OF-WAR

Take a short length of strong rope. You hang on to one end and tell the dog to pick up the other. A knot in his end will help him get a good grip.

Pull playfully on the rope,

saying "Hang on to it! Pull!" If he tries to race around and play with the rope, make him "Stay" and concentrate the play in a limited area.

Gradually, as the dog gets your meaning, you can tug harder, and in a very short time you find yourself in a real tug-of-war. When you've had your fun and want to call it quits, say

Don't attempt this trick until the puppy has a strong back. For smaller breeds wait until the dog is at least six months old, and the larger breeds, from nine months to a year. Some breeds don't ever have the body build to sit up succesfully. You'll be able to gauge your pet's potential by the way he holds his back during the first tries.

Not only can you teach your dog to play tug-of-war with you, but you can teach him to play this game with other dogs as well.

"Drop it !" in a firm, serious tone, and make sure that he obeys at once.

BEGGING

We're calling this "Begging" rather than "Sitting up" to avoid confusion with the obedience command "Sit!" For this the cue can be either "Beg!" or "Up!" Choose whichever you prefer, then stick to it.

Here again, as in shaking hands, a puppy will instinctively rise to his hind feet in play. When he does, grasp his paws and gently push him back on his rump. Hold him erect and try to get him to balance himself. A finger held a bit above his nose will help him to focus his attention and gain balance. When you sense that he is resting squarely on his rump, remove all support except one hand. Then let this hand move slowly away until you're supporting him by just one finger; finally, remove any assistance altogether. At the same time keep commanding "Beg!"

If this doesn't work, try taking him to a corner of the room and giving the order to sit. If he has not been trained to sit on command, press down on his hindquarters until he sits naturally in the angle of the walls that serves as support. Hold his favorite toy or treat over his head until he rises on his hind feet. With your free hand, gently take a paw and set him back on his haunches. Command him to "Beg" as you help him establish his balance. Let him sniff the treat all the time you are talking. Reward and praise. Repeat several times a day for a few minutes each session. A good time is just before a meal when the dog is sure to be hungry. Do not, however, let him work without the supporting walls until he has learned to balance himself well. Once he gets the idea, he'll start sitting up without the command just to gain your attention.

Also known as sitting up, when in the proper begging position the dog should rise to his hind feet and sit back on his haunches.

Many dog owners prefer their dog to beg for something rather than to "Speak" for it. It's less startling and much cuter. When he has learned to "Beg"braced in the corner, try commanding him to beg while he's sitting squarely on the floor. He'll recognize the word but the situation will be different: his front feet are down. Gently raise him. He'll be expecting something like this and his backbone will stiffen.

Give him loads of praise even for holding himself erect only a few seconds.

STAND UP AND WALK

First your dog must be taught to stand up. Hold a treat above his nose and encourage him to rear up on his hind legs. Repeat the command "Stand up" as he reaches for the food.

If he jumps up and down, give him a "No . . . No" and repeat "Stand up." If necessary support his front paws with your free hand.

As soon as he remains erect for an instant, say "All right" and give him a treat. Never let

For small breeds, such as the Schipperke, you should not attempt to teach begging until the dog is at least six months of age and his back is strong enough for this type of trick.

An Italian Greyhound sails through a tire jump at an agility trial. Although generally considered lap dogs, with proper training some toy breeds do well in agility competitions and the like.

CLIMB A LADDER

The steps of the ladder should be wide. Lean it against a low roof so that the dog will find some kind of a landing place when he gets to the top. Do not put any treat at the top because in his haste to reach it he may fall and, if he hurts himself, may lose self confidence or may die a senseless death.

A ball, held in your hand just in front of the dog's nose, can govern his speed. The top of the ladder should be within your reach.

Work without a leash. Tell him to "Climb" and encourage him by "Go on," guiding his feet from one step to the next. Every time he gains a step or two, say "That's right!"

German Shepherd climbing a ladder. For the first few tries you may need to guide your dog up the ladder by *gently* holding on to his collar.

him get at the food by grabbing it. Make him sit normally while you reward him.

A harness sometimes helps with this. Steady him with a leash attached to the chest strap. But be careful not to unbalance him. If he shows any inclination to stand without the aid of a leash, don't use one.

After he has learned to stand on his hind feet with ease, say "Walk" as you back away, a few steps at a time, holding the treat slightly above him. Discourage everything but walking.

Do not be unreasonable and keep the dog standing or walking for any length of time.

If he tries to mount too fast say "Take it easy." Praise him when he gets to the top even if you have helped him. Reward him and let him rest for a minute before starting down. If he seems timid, climb up to him and help him overcome his fear by comforting him. Then start down first and help him by guiding his feet step by step. When he reaches the bottom reward him. Repeat. He will soon climb with assurance.

JUMPING THROUGH A HOOP

Get a hoop large enough to give the dog ample space to sail through. It should be large enough, at the beginning, so he will not strike the sides or the top when jumping. If it is a metal or rough wooden hoop, better wrap it with strips of rags, so the dog will not strike the sharp edges in his first efforts. Later on, he will have the wisdom to take care of himself; but while teaching him, make everything easy and pleasant.

Use a long leash or rope. Bring the free end through the hoop and coil it in your hands until the dog is about three feet away. Tell him to "Sit . . . Stay!" With your free hand, hold the hoop about a foot from him. Say "Jump through the hoop!" and assist him by pulling on the leash. Use a warm, inviting tone. After he has been helped through, reward and pet him. Repeat until he begins to get the idea.

A smooth Collie jumping through a hoop. The hoop you use should be large enough so that the dog will not strike the sides or top when going through it.

In later lessons, have an assistant hold the hoop about five feet from the dog while you back to the end of the leash and call him to you with the cue "Jump through the hoop!" Be sure he "Stays" until you call him, and that you say "All right" and reward him when he has performed satisfactorily.

SCENT DISCRIMINATION

Scent discrimination is one of the exercises included in advanced obedience training. However, it is a spectacular trick in itself—one well worth the effort of teaching even if you do not intend to go in for Obedience Trial work. In this exercise the dog goes to a miscellaneous collection of objects (wood, leather and metal) and chooses the one—and only the one—that you have previously handled. The remaining articles must either be sterile or have been handled by someone other them, and give you several.

These you are to handle a great deal, rub, and carry around in your pocket. The others are to remain in his possession. If you must prepare the clothespins yourself, wash them well in soap and water, rinse and dry, and drop them into a plastic bag, using tongs or pliers to do so. All

In scent discrimination, the dog must go to a miscellaneous collection of objects and choose the one—and only the one—that you have previously handled.

than yourself.

It follows then that the best way to teach this exercise is with an assistant. He can handle the articles that you are not, under any circumstances, to touch. (If you do attempt the training alone, use kitchen tongs, pliers, or rubber gloves to keep from getting your scent on the objects.)

Your dog must, of course, know how to fetch before he can be taught scent discrimination.

Start with wooden articles. Clothespins are about the right size. Paint them different colors or have your assistant number articles handled one day should be boiled or washed before the next lesson.

Start by using only two pins; one with your scent on it; one that has been handled only by your assistant. He puts his pin on the floor (or ground) about 15 feet from the dog whom you have placed in a "Stay" position. Show the dog your pin, let him sniff it, but do not let him take it into his mouth—your scent, not his, should be on it.

With your dog at "Stay," let him watch you go over to place your clothespin beside the other. Go back to him and cup the palm of your hand over his nose, allowing him to smell it. Now say "Fetch" or "Get it!" If he has learned his "fetching" well, he will go to the two pins, sniff them, and pick out the one you have put there. If he picks the right one (you can identify it by the color or number) praise him, and encourage him to return to you and sit facing you. After a second or so say "Give," and accept the pin.

Repeat. However you can not use the clothespin he has already carried in his mouth. Handle a fresh one each time. Praise him as soon as he picks up the right one, shame him if he chooses wrong. Make him drop it, and indicate the right one. That and that only is the one he is to retrieve.

When he has learned to discriminate between two clothespins, increase the number, one at a time, but remember each time that all but one must be sterile: neither his scent nor yours on them.

After he has learned to discriminate between wooden articles you can go on to leather ones, and finally metal ones. The leather can be an old glove, wallet or shoe tongue rolled into a tight cylinder and taped with a thong. The metal can be tubing cut into short lengths, or metal hair rollers.

Only after the dog has learned to select correctly from each of the three groups should all groups be scrambled together for the final, spectacular test.

Whippet performing scent discrimination in advanced obedience training. Even if you don't intend to go in for Obedience Trial work, it is a fun trick to teach your dog.

OVER THE TOP

Choose a hurdle that is not spiked or slippery on the top. It must not be too high: at the beginning no higher than the dog's shoulder. After a few weeks it can be raised to twice his height.

Don't, at any point of jump training, be tempted to see how high your dog can go. He can overexert and strain himself badly. The muscles must be developed gradually. No small breed of dog should be allowed to jump until it is at least eight months old, and no large breed until it is over a year.

Yellow Labrador clearing the bar jump at an agility trial. An agility trial is an obstacle course for dogs designed to test their coordination and intelligence.

Your tone is the incentive in teaching your dog to jump. Make him "Stay!" six or eight feet from the hurdle, while you take your place on the other side, with the end of a long leash (or rope) in your hand. As you tell him "Over the top!" in an encouraging tone, give him a start with the aid of the leash. Take up most of the slack, but do not attempt to drag him over. If he stops on his side of the hurdle, go up close to it, and say "Come on!" "Over the top!" and assist him over the top of the hurdle.

Use the leash only to keep him from running around the end of the hurdle. If necessary, help him over with your hands while coaxing and assuring him that it is the thing to do. When he gains your side of the barrier, reward him. Then order him to "Stay" while you return to the other side by jumping over the hurdle yourself. Position yourself, again

Once you have taught your dog to jump over hurdles you may want to add a new dimension to this trick. This Golden is going over a high jump carrying a Gumadisc®.

say "Over the top!" and repeat the exercise, back and forth, until the dog begins to understand.

OTHER TRICKS

Most dog tricks actually take advantage of the animal's own impulses. We see him do something that looks amusing, perhaps a yawn, or stretch, or chasing his tail. Assign a definite command to the action and every time the dog does it, call out the cue, give him a treat and pet him to show that you are pleased. Once the cue has become associated with the trick, you will be able to issue the command, and have the animal respond.

HOW NOT TO TRAIN A DOG

DO NOT begin to instruct your puppy in anything but

Border Collie leaping over the broad jump. Remember, your tone of voice is the incentive in teaching your dog to jump.

house manners until it is at least four months old.

DO NOT be careless with your words and gestures. Always use the same word and gesture for each command. Be precise.

DO NOT work a dog without a leash for the first few months. At times a person will find himself pressed for time and neglect to put on the collar and leash. Better to forgo the lesson than

DO NOT keep any tidbits you are using as a reward in sight. Carry them in a pocket where you can get at them quickly. Food nearby distracts a dog and he will not give you his full attention.

DO NOT yell at your dog. Use plenty of inflection but never shout or stamp your feet.

DO NOT lose your temper. If you cannot control yourself, you

The Gumabone® Frisbee®* is so soft that it doesn't hurt you, your dog, or anything else it might accidentally strike. This makes it an ideal toy for training or just plain fun.
The trademark Frisbee is used under license from Mattel, Inc., California, USA.

give it hastily.

DO NOT work a dog over 15 minutes at a time. Never let the lesson become monotonous.

DO NOT let anyone but yourself give the dog a command until he has learned the lesson. It is bad for more than one person to teach a dog. Each trainer has his own mannerisms and tones and the dog becomes accustomed to these.

DO NOT hold unnecessary conversation with another person during the lesson. Let the command you are teaching be the only word the dog hears.

DO NOT let anyone else feed the dog when you are training him.

cannot control your dog. This is particularly true when you are attempting to entertain an audience. Wait until he has learned his lessons well before you start showing him (and yourself) off.

DO NOT use a whip, stick, leash, or chain to punish a dog. You want your pet to learn because he loves you, not because he fears you. Punish him only when absolutely necessary by taking hold of the loose skin on his neck, just behind the ears, and command his attention while you scold him with your voice and expression.

The possibilities of the tricks that you can teach your dog are endless. This German Shepherd is jumping through a hoop of fire. A task like this should only be attempted by professionals.

SUGGESTED READING

The following books are all published by T.F.H. Publications, Inc. and are recommended to you for additional information:

Successful Dog Training by Michael Kamer (TS-205) contains the latest training methods used by professional dog trainers. Author and Hollywood dog trainer Michael Kamer is one of the most renowned trainers in the country, having trained both stunt dogs for movies and house pets for movie stars such as Frank Sinatra, Barbara Streisand, Arnold Schwarzenegger, Sylvester Stallone, and countless others. The most modern techniques of training are presented step-by-step and illustrated with fantastic full-color photography. Whether you are a long time obedience trainer or a new dog owner, *Successful Dog Training* will prove an invaluable tool in developing or improving your own training skills.

Owner's Guide to Dog Health by Lowell Ackerman, D.V.M. (TS-214) is the most comprehensive volume on dog health available today. Internationally respected veterinarian Dr. Lowell Ackerman examines in full detail the signs of illness and disease, diagnosis, treatment and therapy options as well as preventative measures, all in simple terms that are easy for the reader to understand. Hundreds of color photographs and illustrations throughout the

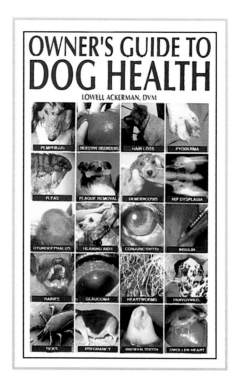

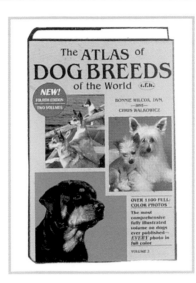

text help to explain the latest procedures and technological advances in all areas of canine care, including nutrition, skin and haircoat care, vaccinations, and more. *Owner's Guide to Dog Health* is an absolute must for those who sincerely care about the health of their dog.

The Atlas of Dog Breeds of the World (H-1091) by Bonnie Wilcox, DVM, and Chris Walkowicz traces the history and highlights the characteristics, appearance and function of every recognized dog breed in the world. 409 different breeds receive full-color treatment and individual study. Hundreds of breeds in addition to those recognized by the American Kennel Club and the Kennel Club of Great Britain are included—the dogs of the world complete! The ultimate reference work, comprehensive coverage, intelligent and delightful discussions. The perfect gift book.

A very successful spinoff of the *Atlas* is *The Mini-Atlas of Dog Breeds*, written by Andrew DePrisco and James B. Johnson. This compact but comprehensive book has been praised and recommended by most national dog publications for its utility and reader-friendliness. The true field guide for dog lovers.

Canine Lexicon by Andrew DePrisco and James Johnson, (TS-175) is an up-to-date encyclopedic dictionary for the dog person. It is the most complete single volume on the dog ever published covering more breeds than any other book as well as other relevant topics, including health, showing, training, breeding, anatomy, veterinary terms, and much more. No dog book before has ever offered this many stunning color photographs of all breeds, dog sports, and topics (over 1300 in full color).

In addition to the foregoing, the following dog training books of

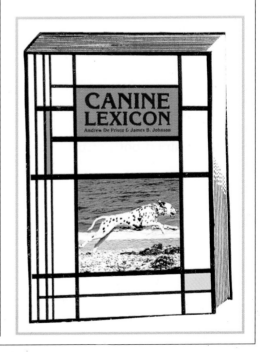

interest to readers of this book are available at pet shops and book stores.

Teaching the Family Dog has never been more fun and easy! *Just Say "Good Dog"*, (TS-204), is a new approach in teaching dogs to be good family dogs and good house dogs. This most original manual to canine education by Linda Goodman, author and dog teacher, addresses all the basic commands and day-to-day problems as well as the considerations and responsibilities of dog ownership. Living with a dog should be a rewarding experience, and this book will show you how. Delightful illustrations by AnnMarie Freda accompany the author's fun and anecdotal text to reinforce the importance of a positive approach to dog training. *Just Say "Good Dog"* is both very informative and authoritative, as the author, assisted by Marlene Trunnell, offers many years of experience and know-how.

Lew Burke's Dog Training by Lew Burke (H-962). The purpose of this book is simple: to let readers do for themselves what premier dog trainers like the author would charge hundreds of dollars for. In it Lew Burke—Who has trained dogs for industry and the government and many individual owners in addition to his movie, television and stage appearances—takes readers right into the canine mind. The elements of dog training for *any* purpose are made easy to grasp and easy to apply because of the author's concentration on the thing that really counts: understanding dogs' needs in relation to their owners' needs.

Everybody Can Train Their Own Dog dog by Angela White (TW-113) is a fabulous reference guide for all dog owners. This well written, easy-to-understand book covers all training topics in alphabetical order for instant location. In addition to teaching, this book provides problem solving and problem prevention techniques that are fundamental to training. All teaching methods are based on motivation and kindness, which bring out the best of a dog's natural ability and instinct.